FAMILY HOME EVENING FOR LITTLE ONES

A YEAR OF FHE LESSONS FOR THE YOUNG FAMILY

"The ideal way to transform your home into a house of learning is to hold family home evening faithfully. The Church has reserved Monday evening for that purpose. In 1915, the First Presidency instructed local leaders and parents to inaugurate a home evening, a time when parents should teach their families the principles of the gospel. The Presidency wrote: 'If the Saints obey this counsel, we promise that great blessings will result. Love at home and obedience to parents will increase. Faith will be developed in the hearts of the youth of Israel, and they will gain power to combat the evil influence and temptations which beset them.'"

-Joseph B. Wirthlin, Apr. 1993 general conference

"We cannot afford to neglect this heaven-inspired program. It can bring spiritual growth to each member of the family, helping him or her to withstand the temptations which are everywhere. The lessons learned in the home are those that last the longest."

-President Thomas S. Monson, "Constant Truths for Changing Times," Apr. 2005 general conference

---

Matthew 19:14 – But Jesus said, suffer little children, and forbid them not, to come unto me: for of such is the kingdom of heaven.

Introduction & Helpful Hints

First and foremost, please feel free to adapt any of these lessons to the needs of your own family. I have chosen what works best for me and my kiddos, but everyone learns in different ways. I hope this will be easy and fun for your family! These lessons/activities are geared towards children aged approximately 0-8 and will take only 15 or 20 minutes to complete. They do not include extensive doctrine or literature but rely mostly on parent led discussion. As your kids grow, you may want to incorporate General Conference talks, scripture reading and more church literature in addition to the activities.

Most lessons do not need to be given in any particular order. There are a few that coincide with certain weeks of the year. They are as follows:

- New Year
- Easter
- General Conference April/October: This lesson has ideas to keep kids reverent and engaged during conference. The FHE on the Mondays following each session are just family discussions about conference.

- Independence Day
- Back to School
- Thanksgiving
- Christmas
- Year End

You might also want to give the lessons titled "I Can Say I'm Sorry" and "I Can Forgive" on weeks back to back.

Some lessons will require a bit more preparation, so you may find it helpful to read lessons through a few days in advance.

The song listed with each lesson is coordinated to the topic of the week. If there is none listed, just choose one of your family's favorites. All songs come from the Children's Songbook. Page numbers are listed and also can be pulled up and played through LDS.org.

All scriptures referenced can also be pulled up on LDS.org. My children like to listen to the songs being played and the scriptures read out loud on our phone or computer.

Some lessons have a coordinating treat idea. If there is no treat listed for the lesson, take a look at the Treat Ideas list included at the beginning of the book for some fun new ideas.

Although there are 52 weeks in a year there are not quite that many lessons included. This is because there are always a few weeks each year when we don't have a lesson and just take a family field trip or have a miscellaneous activity at home. These "field trip" weeks usually coordinate with a holiday/event. Included is a list of our family favorites if you need some ideas.

It's fun for kids to invite friends/neighbors over to be included in FHE once in a while.

Lastly, I hope that your FHE is fun! That is why I created this book. My prayer is that these lesson plans help keep all your little ones happy, feeling included and growing in their knowledge of the love of Christ and the importance of families.

Lessons

Treat Ideas

- Popcorn
- Popsicles
- Homemade Ice Cream
- Smoothies
- Limeade
- Root Beer Floats
- Fresh Berries and Cream
- Watermelon
- Banana Splits
- Milk Shakes
- Ice Cream Sandwiches
- Fondue
- Caramel Corn
- S'mores
- Hot Chocolate
- Homemade Bread
- Scones
- Toast with Nutella and Strawberries/Bananas
- Crepes
- Cookies and Milk
- Veggies and Hummus
- Rice Cereal Treats
- Apples and Cheese

*Preparing the treat in the afternoon is a great way to get children involved and excited for FHE.

Field Trip Ideas

- Christmas lights at temple square
- Sort and donate unused toys or clothing
- Shopping for back-to-school supplies
- Family bike ride
- Pumpkin Patch/Carving
- Baseball game
- Dinner out (great way to practice "Good Manners" lesson)
- Raking leaves
- Sledding/Ice Skating
- Movie night
- Bowling
- Hiking
- Picnic at the park
- Decorate for Holidays
- Dying Eggs
- Make a list of activities you would like to do as a family over summer break
- Cooking/baking
- Visit a local museum
- Visit the elderly
- Deliver snacks or personal hygiene items to the homeless
- Invite missionaries over for dinner
- Write thank-you cards to the children's Primary teachers
- Swimming
- Nature Walk

America the Beautiful

Prayer

Song: #225 – "My Flag, My Flag"

Scripture: Alma 46: 11-17 (Moroni and the title of liberty)

Supplies: Varies depending on activity choice. See list below.

Ask the children why they think we celebrate Independence Day. Discuss as a family the blessings we have because we are privileged to live in a free country. Explain to the children that many people have sacrificed, and continue to do so, to serve and protect our country in order for us to have the freedoms that we do.

Activity Ideas:

1. Discuss the symbolism of the American flag. Give the children craft paper/markers/glue and let them create their own flags.
2. Write/draw thank you cards or purchase snacks to send to soldiers around the world through a program such as Operation Shoebox (www.operationshoebox.com) or Operation Gratitude (www.operationgratitude.com).
3. Bake a cake and decorate with white frosting, blueberries and strawberries to look like the American flag. Enjoy as the treat.

Treat: Homemade ice cream or snow cones.

Armor of God

Prayer

Song: #172 – "We'll Bring the World His Truth"

Scripture: Ephesians 6:11

Supplies: Orange, bowl and water

Activity: Explain what it means to put on the armor of God. Teach the children that when we keep our armor on, Satan cannot harm us. If we take off the armor, even one piece, we can be hurt. Have children place the orange in a bowl of water and see what it does (it should float). Then have them peel the orange a little bit and watch the orange dip lower in the water. Peel a little bit more and watch the orange start to sink even more. Explain that just like the orange was able to stay afloat with its peel or "armor" on, we are able to stay afloat when we put on the armor of God. If we choose not to, we will be more susceptible to temptation and may sink just as the orange did.

Treat: Orange slices or fresh squeezed orange juice

Baptism

Prayer

Song: #103 – "When I Am Baptized"

Scripture: Moroni 7:34

Supplies: Colored paper, scissors, and glue or rainbow printout and crayons

Activity: Lead a discussion on baptism

- Why are we baptized?
- Who baptizes us?
- What happens after we are baptized?
- What do we wear when we are baptized?
- At what age are we baptized?
- What promises do we make when we are baptized?
- What are we promised if we keep our baptismal covenants?

Explain that rainbows are often used as a symbol of baptism because it appears after the earth is washed clean from rain. When we are baptized, our sins are washed away just like the rain cleanses the earth. Let the children cut/paste or color rainbows of their own.

Treat: Skittles

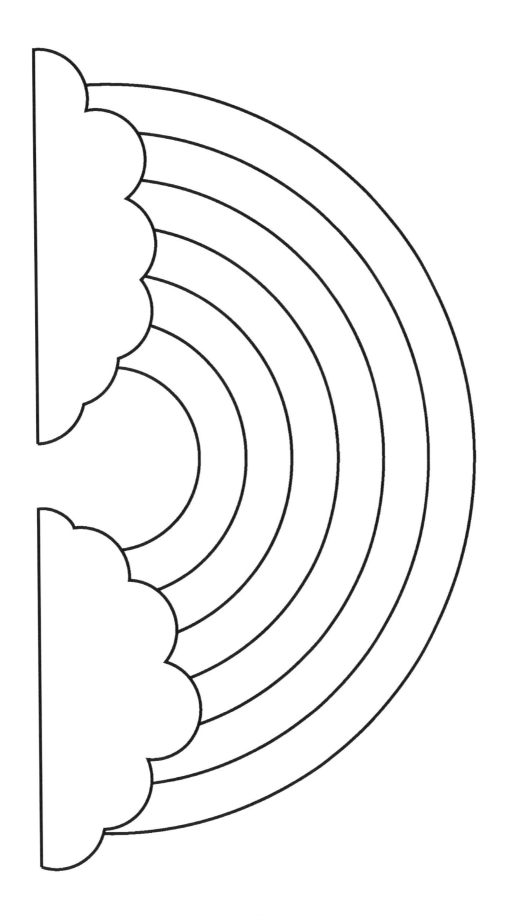

Being Brave

Prayer

Song: #96 – "Faith"

Scripture: Isaiah 41:13

Supplies: Wooden lion masks (found at Dollar Tree or craft stores such as Michaels/Joann's/Hobby Lobby) or lion coloring page and markers/crayons

Activity: Tell the story of Daniel and the lions' den located in Daniel Chapter 6. Ask the children if they think Daniel was afraid of being put into a den with lions. Discuss with the children what some of their fears are. Explain that with the Lords help and faith in Him we can be courageous just like Daniel. The Lord will guide and protect us if we have faith in Him. Let children color in the lion masks or the lion coloring page to remember they can be brave like Daniel.

Treat: Animal crackers

Being Respectful

Prayer

Song: #78 – "I'm Trying to Be Like Jesus"

Scripture: Ephesians 4:28-32

Supplies: T-H-I-N-K and RESPECT printouts

This lesson is all about how to be respectful in and out of the home. The lesson may get broken down into multiple lessons if desired in order to cover the following topics more thoroughly, or if there is one that is more of a struggle in your home.

Activity: Discuss what respect means. Choose one or more of the topics from below and discuss thoroughly using examples. Challenge the family to keep an eye out for people showing respect to others during the week. Make sure to say "thank you" or "great job" to the family member who is being respectful!

- Respecting your parents & siblings
- Respecting your teacher
- No trespassing/touching other peoples' belongings
- No back-talk/sass-mouth
- Waiting patiently/interrupting politely
- Saying please and thank you
- Respecting peoples time/not being late

The two printouts included may be used as aids for the lesson and hung up in the home as a reminder. They also bring a few more specific ways to show respect.

Treat

THINK

BEFORE YOU SPEAK

T – IS IT TRUE?

H – IS IT HELPFUL?

I – IS IT INSPIRING?

N – IS IT NECESSARY?

K – IS IT KIND?

WE CAN SHOW RESPECT BY:

Being honest – Sharing – Waiting our turn – Helping others – Using "Please" and "Thank You" – Keeping our hands to ourselves – Being on time – Using kind words – Obeying our parents and teachers – Cleaning up after ourselves – Being prepared – Doing our best – Following the "golden rule"

Choose the Right

Prayer

Song: #160 – "Choose the Right"

Scripture: Alma 37:35

Supplies: CTR ring/bracelet, gumball machine printout, pom-poms, glue

Activity: Discuss together examples of good choices and bad choices. Take turns talking about good choices you made throughout the past week. Give each child a CTR ring/bracelet* to be a reminder for them to make good choices. Explain how the Lord is pleased when we choose the right. Challenge everyone to put forth extra effort to make right choices this week. When people are observed choosing the right, add a pom-pom to the "chews the right" gumball machine. See if the family can make enough good choices to fill the machine by next week's FHE.

Treat: Gumballs or Hi-"Chews"

* CTR rings/bracelets can both can be found at Deseret Book or the Distribution center. I recommend bracelets for younger children due to the choking hazard.

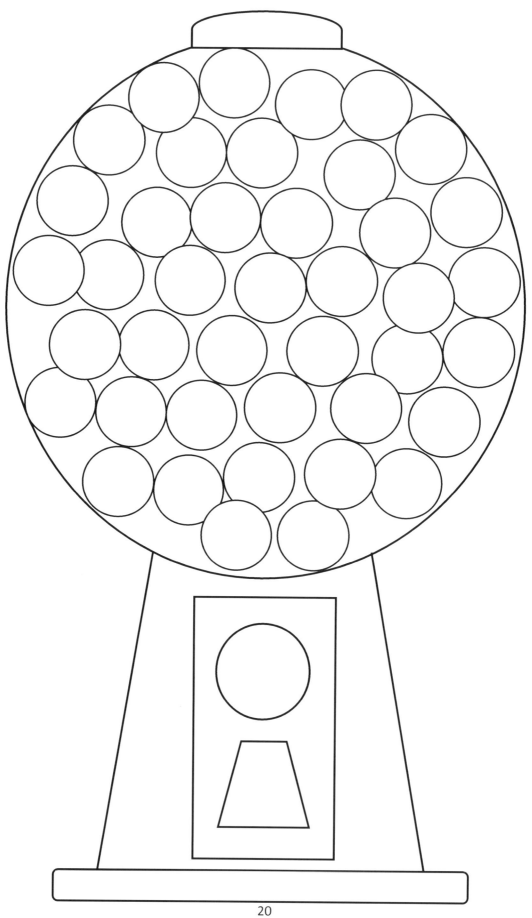

Etiquette Night

Prayer

Song: #256 – "We Welcome You"

Scripture: 1 Corinthians 15:33

Supplies: Food, place settings

Activity: Plan a special dinner for the family*. As a family, teach the children how to correctly set a place setting. Once the table is set, enjoy dinner as usual. During the meal take the time to teach the children proper table manners such as:

- Saying "please" and "thank you" when food is passed
- Waiting your turn
- Sitting still until everyone is finished
- Keeping toys/elbows/feet off the table
- How to say "no thank you" if a menu item is offered that you wouldn't care for
- Asking to be excused when the meal is complete
- Chewing with your mouth closed
- Using a napkin instead of your lap/shirt
- No burping
- Etc.

Treat: Take the kids out for a treat to practice their manners in public**.

* Planning this lesson could be a good Sunday quiet activity. Children might also enjoy accompanying a parent on Monday to select the groceries for your special FHE meal.

**This lesson may also be carried into the following week by taking the family for a dinner out if they practice proper table manners all week. If they are old enough, challenge the children to order their own meals to practice saying please and thank you.

Families Are Forever

Prayer

Song: #188 – "Families Can Be Together Forever"

Scripture: D&C 14:7

Supplies: Sugar cubes or marshmallows, glue or toothpicks, paper plates, Temple Picture(s)

Activity: Explain that temples are a sacred place, and in them sacred promises are made. One of these covenants is the sealing ordinance, which allows us to be sealed to our family for eternity if we are faithful and obey the Lord. Show the family pictures of temples. It might be fun to show a picture of your own sealing day or of someone close to them. Then let the children make their own temple out of sugar cubes and glue or marshmallows and toothpicks. Display their temples as a reminder to follow the Lord so they can be worthy to enter into the House of the Lord when they are the appropriate age.

Treat

Family Finance

Prayer

Song: #210 – "Daddy's Homecoming"

Scripture: Malachi 3:10

Supplies: Varies depending on activity choice

Activity: You can use this week in any way you see fit for your family. Some ideas for teaching family finance:

- Implement an allowance system

http://www.onelittleminuteblog.com/2015/02/star-chart-quick-wallet-diy-chore-system-young-kids/

The blog link listed above leads to a fantastic star chart to get young children started on a daily/weekly routine for earning money by doing housework.

- Teach children how to write a check
- Decide as a family a fun outing you would like to save for and create a savings jar
- Choose a family coin jar to collect loose change for future family vacations
- Create spending/saving/tithing banks

Often times small piggy banks can be found at the dollar store or Target for only a few dollars. Having an adult make a cut into the lid of a mason jar or an oatmeal canister also works as an easy and inexpensive bank.

This week's lesson needs to be adapted to your family's individual needs depending on the age of the children and individual family goals.

Treat: Chocolate coins

Family History

Prayer

Song: #204 – "Mother, Tell Me the Story"

Scripture:

"The doctrine of the family in relation to family history and temple work is clear. The Lord in initial revelatory instructions referred to "baptism for *your* dead." Our doctrinal obligation is to our own ancestors. This is because the celestial organization of heaven is based on families. The First Presidency has encouraged members, especially youth and young single adults, to emphasize family history work and ordinances for their own family names or the names of ancestors of their ward and stake members. We need to be connected to both our roots and branches. The thought of being associated in the eternal realm is indeed glorious."

-Elder Quentin L. Cook
April 2014 General Conference

Supplies: Varies depending on activity choice

Activity:

- Interview Grandparents and record their history. This one is really fun! It can take a few weeks if you wish. Record the audio and type it up to keep a written record. You will never regret doing this and children LOVE to hear stories about when older people were their age.
- Field trip to the family history center

- Log into familysearch.org and start/continue your family history
- Show your children their family tree
- Work together as a family to create your family's genealogy wheel to display in the home. I Chart You is a fantastic company to use. http://www.i-chart-you.com/

Treat

Family Motto (New Year)

Prayer

Song: #261 – "Here We Are Together"

Scripture: D&C 93:40

Supplies: Paper & marker

Activity: Write down together the goals you would like to make for the year to help strengthen the family unit and bring more love into the home. Then decide the family motto for the year; one word or short phrase to focus on throughout the year. (Adventure, Find Happiness, Be Brave, Serve Always, Try New Things, etc.) Display in a common area for the remainder of the year.

Treat

Food Storage

Prayer

Song: #237 – "The Prophet Said to Plant a Garden"

Scripture: Genesis 41:35-36

Supplies: Varies depending on activity choice

Activity: Explain to the children the reasoning behind keeping an extra storage of food for emergencies.

- Take inventory of your food storage. Then go on a field trip to the store and purchase items to add to your food storage. Let children help choose items and put away when home.
- Give this lesson in the spring time and start your family garden; plan or plant.

Treat: Make a treat using food storage items or enjoy fresh produce from the store of the same variety you are planting in your garden.

(Preparing For) General Conference April/October

Prayer

Song: #156 – "The Chapel Doors"
       #177 – "Teach Me to Walk in the Light"

Scripture: D&C 88:119, D&C 109:7

Supplies: Varies depending on activity choice

Activity: Discuss the upcoming General Conference.

- Who will be speaking?
- Why do we listen to General Conference?
- What is spoken about?
- Why we listen/watch at home?
- What can we do to feel the spirit?

Prepare for the upcoming General Conference by collecting/purchasing needed items to help children listen reverently. Below is a list of ideas for toddlers to be reverent during General Conference*:

- Pray as a family before watching/listening to Conference together
- Build temples out of blocks/Legos
- Conference journal to write/draw feelings
- Build a fort and watch inside
- Draw the speaker

- Key word treats. Choose treats and label each with a word (temple, prophet, love, Christ, prayer, etc.). Each time the kids hear the word, they get one of the corresponding treats.

Challenge each family member to remember their favorite talk or story from a talk that they can share at next week's FHE.

Treat

*Remember: Children are children and it is OK if you don't get to listen to all of General Conference, or even an entire session, because your little ones need your attention. The Lord only asks that we do our best. The conference talks will be printed in the following month's Ensign that may be purchased at the Distribution Center and are also made available on LDS.org. The conference edition Ensigns are great references to use for FHE lessons.

God Gave Us a Beautiful World

Prayer

Song: #246 – "It's Autumntime"

Scripture: Genesis Chapter 1

Supplies: Empty grocery bag, paper lunch sacks

Activity: After reading the story of the creation of the world, discuss with the children the things they are most grateful for about this earth and what we can do to take care of it. Take the family on a walk. Use the grocery bag to pick up litter and the lunch sacks as the kids own "nature hunt" bag. Let the kids collect items from nature, making sure to explain that we don't pick other people's flowers or harm living plants/animals.

Treat: Bring a treat along on the walk and enjoy it in nature. Granola Bars, apple slices, crackers, trail mix, cheese stick, etc.

Good Friends

Prayer

Song: #145 – "Kindness Begins with Me"

Scripture: Moroni 7:16

Supplies: Cornstarch, water and bowl, or letter writing supplies

Activity: For older children: Ask why it is important to surround ourselves with friends who support us and respect our values.

In a large bowl, mix 1/2 cup of water with 1 cup of cornstarch. Let the kids run the goo through their fingers. Then ask them to take a handful and squeeze tightly. The mixture will become strong. As they release their grip, the mixture will become gooey again and fall through their fingers.

Explain that by surrounding ourselves with good friends, and holding tight to our values, we become strong. But if we choose to let go of our values and surround ourselves with friends who don't support us, we become weak; just like the cornstarch became weak when we didn't hold tight. Explain that good friends can come from different backgrounds and worship different religions as long as they respect us for who we are and encourage us to be good people.

For younger children: Discuss attributes of a good friend. Let each child write or draw a picture to send to one of their friends thanking them for being a good friend.

Treat

Good Manners

Prayer

Song: #78 – "I'm Trying to Be Like Jesus"

Scripture: 1 Corinthians 15:33

Supplies: Dinosaur figures (Check Target or Dollar Tree)

Activity: Read the following story using the dinosaur toys as the characters.

My Journey to Dino-Land

A long time ago in a land far, far away I met some unusual dinosaurs whose manners had gone away…

First, I met Sassy-Stegosaurus. She is sharp and sassy. She thinks she should always be first in line, take the first turn on the playground, be first one to eat; it's always about her. She acts like she is the only one that's important. She turns green with envy if you have something that she wants. And she gets mad unless she gets her way; Pouting and whining until people give her what she wants. The other dinosaurs didn't want to play with her anymore because she bossed everyone around. She was making everyone else feel miserable, including me, so I went on my way…

Next, I came upon an Angry-Ankylosaurus. Now he's okay to be around as long as he is in a good mood; he is one swell pal. But if he woke up on the wrong side of the bed, you better watch out because he gets all fired up. He yells at his sisters when they take his toys, screams at his Momma when she makes him eat his vegetables and hits his friends when they don't play what he wants. I started to see steam coming from Angry-Ankylosaur's ears so I knew it was time to scram...

I had to duck down fast, because no sooner than I had left, down swooped Tattle -Pterodactyl! She is always on the lookout for something or someone to tattle on. She doesn't play with the others a lot because she is too busy trying to catch them doing something wrong. When she sees something she doesn't like, she hurriedly flies away to find a grown-up to tell. And nothing is EVER her fault. When the dinosaurs start to argue she is the first to run and tattle, even though she is part of the problem sometimes too. I didn't want her tattling on me so I went on my way...

All of the sudden I could hear this terrible noise. It was Vulgar-Velociraptor and boy was he noisy! You could hear him wherever he was and his words weren't pretty. His Daddy had asked him to stop using potty talk but he kept calling his sisters yucky words. He told his friends to shut-up and shouted "NO" when his parents asked him to help around the house. He even called me a naughty word so I left as quickly as I could...

The next dinosaur I saw was big and tall. I was scared by his size at first but his manners were even scarier! Rude-Rex was his name. He doesn't think it's important to say please or thank you. He doesn't ask permission. He never says excuse me and he interrupts everyone. He takes whatever he wants and he even grabbed my sandwich right out of my hand! He doesn't have any table manners and burps real loud because he thinks it's funny. He was about ready to burp again when I ran for cover. Dinosaur burps are especially smelly...

Oh No! Next came Pouty-Plateosaurus. Shhhh! You have to be really careful what you say around her because she gets her feelings hurt super easy. She is always discouraged about something. She gets upset because she says she can't draw as well as everyone else or because she can't read as quickly. She gets her feelings hurt if someone can't have a play date or if it rains and her soccer games are cancelled. Pouty-Plateosaurus never seems happy. A storm cloud was coming and I knew she would start pouting about getting wet so I said goodbye and kept on walking...

As I was walking I quickly caught up to Tardy-Triceratops. She was walking to dance class but was running late. She is always late. She pokes around until the last minute and then she can't catch up. Her Momma has to call her and call her to get her out of bed in the morning. She is always the last one dressed, the last one to finish eating and the last one out the door. She's the last one to school, the last one to dinner; she's even late to play dates. I didn't want to make her even tardier for class so I bid farewell...

Well, it sure had been a long day! I was feeling grumpy and sad after meeting all these beautiful dinosaurs that had ugly manners. Then I saw it, the most beautiful dinosaur of all. It had a smile on it like you wouldn't believe. I quickly ran up to it to introduce myself. I learned that he was the Happy-Osaurus. And that he is friends with everyone. He is courteous and friendly. He never interrupts and he is always willing to share. He rarely tattles or whines. Sometimes Happy-Osaurus still gets sad or upset just like everyone else, but he isn't rude. He uses kind words to tell others how he is feeling. And he feels really badly when he is late, making others wait for him. Happy-Osaurus makes mistakes sometimes too but is quick to say he is sorry and forgive those who have hurt him. His happiness was contagious and I immediately felt better about myself. Happy-Osaurus knows he is special and made me feel special too. I sure hope that you're lucky enough to have a lot of Happy-Osaurs living in your house. The End.

Treat: Dinosaur fruit snacks

Grateful NOT Greedy

Prayer

Song: #6 - "Thanks to Thee"

Scripture: Psalm 147:7

Supplies: Old magazines, glue, poster board, scissors

Activity: Discuss what our wants vs. needs are. Cut out pictures from magazines of things we want and things we need. Glue them onto different halves of the poster board and display for the week to remind the family to be grateful for the things we have/need; not greedy for items we want. Explain to the kids that it is OK to want fun things, but they shouldn't expect them or whine when they don't get everything they want. Also, remind them that when they do get a "want" item, that they should use proper manners and say "Thank You" or write a thank you note to show their gratefulness.

Treat

Hard Work and Helpful Hands

Prayer

Song: #198 – "When We're Helping"

Scripture: Proverbs 22:6

Supplies: Varies depending on activity choice. See list below.

Activity: Growing up we had many of these lessons. This is an easy one to throw together on a week when time seems to be getting away from us and you need a lesson in a pinch. We were raised that if you live in the home, you help keep it. This week teach the children a new household chore that they haven't learned yet.

Examples include:

- Mowing the lawn
- Washing the kitchen table/chairs
- Cleaning toilets
- Separating garbage and recyclables
- Loading/unloading the dishes
- Vacuuming
- Sorting/washing/folding laundry
- Weeding (weeds vs. plants)
- Washing the car
- Changing a tire
- Changing the oil
- Wiping walls
- Sanitizing toys

These can all be adapted as needed depending on ages.

Treat: On "job nights" my Dad usually treated us to milkshakes...just an option.

Helpful Hearts

Prayer

Song: #198 – "When We're Helping"

Scripture: D&C 4:2

Supplies: Clay

Activity: Discuss how helping others can make our hearts feel happy as well as makes the Lord happy. Make clay hearts. During the following week, challenge each family member to do simple acts of service for one another and leave a clay heart in the spot where the service was performed. See how long the "helping heart" chain continues.

Treat: Heart-shaped treat

Note** The Crayola clay does not dry. Make sure to purchase a brand that can be air dried or baked to harden.

Honesty

Prayer

Song: #149 – "I Believe in Being Honest"

Scripture: 13th Article of Faith

Supplies: Book, *The Empty Pot* by Demi (You can borrow this book from your local library but I highly recommend purchasing a copy for your home library. It sells for under $10 on Amazon.com)

Activity: Read *The Empty Pot.* Discuss what it means to be honest and (if the children are old enough) what integrity means. Explain that being honest means not telling lies but also means not withholding truth and not cheating or stealing. Explain to the children that being honest is not always the easy thing to do, sometimes it is actually very difficult, but that by being honest we will be blessed, gain individual strength and feel more at peace.

Treat

I Am a Child of God

Prayer

Song: #2 – "I Am a Child of God"

Scripture: Galatians 3:26 & Romans 8:16

Supplies: Small box with a mirror inside.

Activity: Read the following paragraph from "The Family: A Proclamation to the World":

> "ALL HUMAN BEINGS—male and female—are created in the image of God. Each is a beloved spirit son or daughter of heavenly parents, and, as such, each has a divine nature and destiny."

Tell each child that there is a picture of one of the most important people in the entire world inside the box. Let them guess who they think it is. After they all guess, let each member of the family look inside the box in the mirror. Explain that we are all children of God and we were created in his image, that we all have unique talents, physical features and no two people are the same but we are ALL important!

Treat

I Can Forgive

Prayer

Song: #99 – "Help Me, Dear Father"

Scripture: Matthew 5:44

Supplies: Rocks or canned food, backpack

Activity: Ask family members how it feels when others hurt us or make us mad or sad. As each child mentions something, add a rock to the backpack. Once the backpack is nice and full, let each child have a turn wearing it and walking around the house. Once everyone has had their turn, explain to the children that when people hurt our feelings and we stay mad, it can feel heavy and keep us from being happy. Ask the children what we can do when people hurt us. Have the children practice saying, "I forgive you." As they say this let them take an object out of the backpack. Once the pack is empty again, let the children try it on and walk around. Explain that the Lord will lighten our load through forgiveness, and we should do the same for others. Forgiving makes us happy.

Treat

I Can Say I'm Sorry

Prayer

Song: #148 – "I Want to Live the Gospel"

Scripture: Helaman 4:15

Supplies: ABC's of an apology printout

Activity: Have the family gather for FHE. When you walk in, accidentally bump into someone. Immediately apologize for doing so. After you sit down, ask the wrong person to say the weekly FHE prayer. Apologize for the mistake.

After the prayer, song and scripture, ask if any of the family members have a guess as to what this week's lesson is about. If no one guesses correctly point out your mistakes prior to the start of FHE. Explain that you should apologize for your mistakes when they are accidental, but you also need to apologize for when you make the wrong choice.

Discuss some things that have happened in the past week (or make up scenarios) where an apology would be necessary and appreciated. Review the steps of an apology using the ABCD printout. Display in your home for the week as a reminder for the kids. Let each member of the family practice saying "I'm sorry."

With the little ones, I have noticed an improvement when they are reassured that a parent can walk with them to apologize to someone if they feel uncomfortable doing it alone.

Treat

The ABC's of an Apology

A - Admit

B – Be Sorry

C – Confess & Fix

D – Don't Do It Again

I Love to See the Temple

Prayer

Song: #95 – "I Love to See the Temple"

Scripture: D&C 84:4

Activity: Visit your nearest temple. Answer questions your children may have about the temple.

Conversation starters:

- How many temples are there?
- What happens in the temple?
- How old do you need to be to enter the temple?
- What do the symbols on the temple mean?
- Who is the statue of on top of some temples?

Treat

Jesus Looks like Me

Prayer

Song: #55 – "Jesus Once Was a Little Child"

Scripture: Luke 24:39

Supplies: Sidewalk chalk or butcher paper, photo of Christ as a child

Activity: Show the photo of Christ to your children and explain that Jesus was once a child like them, and because he has been resurrected, he has a body of flesh and blood just like we do. Trace each person with sidewalk chalk or on butcher paper. Then let the children color their tracings in or draw what they think Christ looked like as a little child.

Treat

Keep the Sabbath Day Holy

Prayer

Song: #196 – "Saturday"

Scripture: Mosiah 13:16

Supplies: Ice cream sundae supplies, wooden craft sticks

Activity: Dish a bowl of ice cream and place multiple toppings on the counter including "unique" sundae toppings such as mustard or ketchup. Let each family member choose a topping and add it to the sundae. When it is your turn, put on one of the unique toppings. Then offer each person a spoon to share the sundae. Hopefully the kids don't want to eat the ice cream covered in mustard/ketchup/relish.

Explain that just as some toppings don't belong on an ice cream sundae, there are also activities that don't belong on the Sabbath. Discuss activities that would be appropriate on Sunday as well as those that are better saved for later in the week. Write the Sunday activities on the wooden craft sticks and store in a can/jar for the children to choose from if they are having trouble being reverent on the Sabbath.

Treat: Ice cream sundaes - without mustard or relish ;)

Love at Home (Valentine's)

Prayer

Song: #61 – "Jesus Said Love Everyone"

Scripture: John 13:34

Supplies: Sticky notes, photo of each family member, tape

Activity: Tape up a photo of each family member on the wall. Take turns writing down reasons you love them on a sticky note and hang them around each photo. Leave up for the week. Have extra sticky notes on hand to add to the love wall.

Treat: Heart-shaped treat

Missionary Work

Prayer

Song: #169 – "I Hope They Call Me on a Mission"

Scripture: D&C 42:6

Supplies: *Book of Mormon*, letter writing supplies

Activity:

- Write testimonies (kids can draw) to include with the copy of the *Book of Mormon*. As a family, decide who to share it with. Deliver or mail.
- Write letters to a missionary.
- Invite an inactive or nonmember family over for dinner and FHE.
- Have the missionaries over for dinner and ask them to share their testimonies.

Treat

Nativity (Christmas)

Prayer

Song: #50 – "Picture a Christmas"

Scripture: Luke 2

Supplies: Nativity set or costumes

Activity: Have children act out or re-tell the story of the birth of Christ using themselves as characters or using the nativity set.

Treat

Obedience

Prayer

Song: #58 – "Little Lambs So White and Fair"

Scripture: Romans 5:19

Supplies: Ghost printable (cut-out and colored), wooden craft sticks (which are glued to the ghosts)

Activity: Read the following story.

The 5 Little Ghosts

Once upon a time there lived 5 little ghosts. As everyone knows, ghosts are white. To stay white the only thing they can eat is vanilla ice cream and the only thing that they can drink is milk. One day when Mommy Ghost went to the refrigerator there was no vanilla ice cream and no milk left for her baby ghosts so she had to go to the grocery store. Before she left she told her little ghosts, "No matter how hungry you get, do not eat anything until I come home or something horrible will happen."

The first ghost became very thirsty. He looked in the refrigerator and saw a little glass of grape juice and thought, "Just one teeny sip wouldn't hurt." So, he took one teeny sip of grape juice and...he turned purple! The other ghosts looked at him and said, "Mommy told us that something horrible would happen and she was right." The little ghost did not want his mommy to see him all purple, so he ran upstairs and hid in the toy chest.

The second ghost became so hungry that she just had to look in the refrigerator for something to eat. She saw a carrot and thought, "Just one teeny bite wouldn't hurt." So, she took a one teeny bite of the crunchy carrot and...she turned orange! The other ghosts looked at her and said, "Mommy told us that something horrible would happen and she was right." The little ghost did not want her mommy to see her all orange, so she ran upstairs and hid in the bedroom closet.

The third ghost became hungry too and took a look in the refrigerator. He saw a bowl of spinach and thought, "Just one teeny bite wouldn't hurt." So, he took a one teeny bite of spinach and...he turned green! The other ghosts looked at him and said, "Mommy told us that something horrible would happen and she was right." The little ghost did not want his mommy to see him all green, so he ran upstairs and hid under his bed.

The fourth ghost's tummy started to growl because he was hungry too. He thought he would check again for some milk but when he looked in the refrigerator and saw a bowl of strawberries he thought, "Just one teeny bite wouldn't hurt." So, he took a one teeny bite of a strawberry and...he turned red! The other ghost looked at him and said, "Mommy told us that something horrible would happen and she was right." The little ghost did not want his mommy to see him all red, so he ran upstairs and hid behind the playroom door.

The fifth ghost said, "I'm so hungry, but I will not do what my brothers and sister did. I'll look in the freezer and see if there is just maybe a little vanilla ice cream left." When he looked in the freezer, there was some ice cream....and it was almost vanilla - it was chocolate chip ice cream. So, the ghost said, "This shouldn't hurt me - those chocolate chips are so tiny." So, he ate one spoonful and...became a chocolate chip ghost! He certainly didn't want his mommy to see him all spotty, so he ran upstairs and hid in the bathtub.

When Mommy ghost returned she knew something was wrong when she didn't see her children. Mommy ghost started looking for the little ghosts. She found the first one upstairs in the toy chest; a second one in the closet; the third one under the bed; the fourth one behind the door; and the last little ghost in the bathtub. When she found all of them she said, "Little ghosts, I told you that something horrible would happen, and it did. Whatever will we do to get you white again for Halloween?" Mommy Ghost called the doctor and this is what he told her to do. Keep all the little ghosts in bed for three days and give them nothing but vanilla ice cream and milk to eat. If you do this, they should be ready and all white again for Halloween. So that is what she did.

By Halloween night the five little ghosts were happy to be all white again to go out spooking and shouting "BOO!". And from that day on they listened to their Mommy and never again ate something they shouldn't. The End!

Discuss how the ghosts felt when they disobeyed, embarrassed and sad, and how we can feel if we choose the right.

Treat: Chocolate chips

Our Prophet

Prayer

Song: #19 (Hymn Book) – "We Thank Thee O God for a Prophet"

Scripture: Genesis Chapter 6-8: The Story of Noah's Ark.

Supplies: Photo of the Prophet, picture of Noah and the Ark, empty box or laundry basket, stuffed animals.

Activity: After reading the story of Noah, explain to the children that God has called prophets to help guide us for many, many years. Talk about why we have a prophet today, and where he gets the revelation he does to guide and teach us. Explain that the prophet helps deliver messages to us from the Lord, and we should follow his teachings; just as the people on the Ark followed Noah. Take turns playing follow the leader. Once everyone has had a turn, challenge the family to follow the prophet just as they followed the leader in the game. Then let the kids collect stuffed animals to fill the box ("ark") and re-enact the story of Noah's Ark.

Treat

Prayer

Prayer

Song: #12 – "A Child's Prayer"

Scripture: Matthew 21:22

Supplies: Rocks, craft paint, paintbrushes

Activity: Discuss what a prayer is, including how we pray, when we pray, what we pray for, and why we pray. Then decorate your "prayer rocks." Place them on your pillow after you make your bed in the morning to remind you to pray in the morning and remove it at night after you have said your bedtime prayer. also like to leave some in random places around the house (bathroom shelf, laundry room, kitchen window sill) to remind me to pray.

Treat

Priesthood Blessing (Beginning of School Year)

Prayer

Song: Your choice

Scripture: D&C 107:18

Activity: Discuss when priesthood blessings are given and by whom they can be given. Ask the children why they think blessings are given. Talk about each child's baby blessing and any other times in their lives when they have received blessings by their father or other priesthood holder. Re-read the children's baby blessing if you have them written down.

I assigned this lesson at the beginning of the school year because our family tradition has always been to receive a father's blessing the Monday before starting school in the fall.

Treat

Resurrection (Easter)

Prayer

Song: #82 – "When He Comes Again"

Scripture: Matthew 28:6

Supplies: E-A-S-T-E-R egg kit: See supplies list below or various kits can be purchased online.

Activity: Learn about the resurrection of Christ using the scriptures/symbols inside the E-A-S-T-E-R egg kit.

E-A-S-T-E-R Egg Kit Supplies:

- 6 count egg carton with 6 plastic eggs
- Scripture reference slips (see next page)
- Items for each egg as follows:
    - E – Heart sticker/cut-out/trinket
    - A – Band-aid
    - S – Nail
    - T – Rock
    - E – Piece of Gauze
    - R – Nothing. For He is Risen!

E is for Each of us. God loves everyone. - John 13:34

A is for A broken world, so God send His Son. - John 3:15-17

S is for Sacrifice. Christ sacrificed for all our sins - Mark 14:32-36

T is for the Tomb where Christ was laid. - Matthew 27:59-60

E is for Empty, when the stone was rolled away. - Luke 24:1-5

R is for Resurrected. Our Redeemer lives! - Matthew 28:5-6

Treat: Easter egg candy

Reverence

Prayer

Song: #26 – "Reverently, Quietly"

Scripture: D&C 68:29

Supplies: Mr. Potato Head

Activity: Discuss why we are reverent in church. Explain that being reverent doesn't only mean being quiet. Take turns putting body parts on Mr. Potato Head and discussing how we can show reverence with that body part when we are in holy places.

Treat

Safety & Preparedness

Prayer

Song: #281 – "The Wise Man and the Foolish Man"

Scripture: Proverbs 13:20

Supplies: Varies depending on your needs.

Activity: Update family 72-Hour kits. Replace clothing and diapers that are too small, expired food, and add a few dollars.

Go over with the children the safety protocol in case of fire/earthquake, a meeting place if separated, a code word for stranger danger, and help children memorize their address/phone number. As children get older, show them where the emergency gas/water shut off is and how to turn them off.

Treat

Serving Others

Prayer

Song: #174 – "Called to Serve"

Scripture: Mosiah 2:17

Supplies: Varies depending on activity choice. See list below.

Activity: This week is a service project of your choosing.

- Volunteer
- Bring a meal
- Rake leaves
- Shovel snow
- Visit the elderly
- Clean toys in the nursery
- Invite the missionaries for dinner

Happy serving!

Treat: Soft "serve" ice cream

Sibling Appreciation

Prayer

Song: #152 – "Hum Your Favorite Hymn"

Scripture: John 15:12

Supplies: Super hero capes (I made mine; but I have seen many listings on Etsy, or you check Kid to Kid or local second-hand stores)

Activity: Challenge your children to be "super siblings." Hang super hero capes up at a child level where they can be visible. During the week, when you or one of your children see another child being nice/serving one of their siblings, thank them for being a "super sibling." Then let them wear the super hero cape for an allotted amount of time.

Treat

Taking Care of our Bodies

Prayer

Song: #275 – "Head, Shoulders, Knees and Toes"

Scripture: D&C Section 89

Supplies: Smoothie ingredients

Activity: Family exercise night. Take a walk, bike ride, go for a swim or do yoga. Explain that our bodies are special and what we can do to take care of them. Discuss why we eat healthy and exercise and what the Lord has asked us not to eat and drink.

Treat: Green Smoothie

Recipe

- 1 C. Spinach
- 1 C. Water/Milk/Juice
- 1/2 Avocado
- 1 C. Frozen Pineapple/Mangos/Berries
- 1 Banana

Tattling

Prayer

Song: Your Choice

Scripture: Alma 53:20

Supplies: Small box, decorating supplies, Tattling vs. Reporting printout, and a small pad of paper or Post-it notes

Activity: Discuss the differences between tattling and reporting. Give examples of both until the children can tell the difference. Decorate the small box like a "tattle monster," cutting a hole in it for a mouth. Challenge the children to only come to you when something needs to be reported. If it is tattling, they can write/draw their problem on a piece of paper and feed it to the tattle monster. For younger kids who need help being reminded, if they come to you to tattle assist them in writing the tattle down to feed to the tattle monster.

Treat: Monster Rice Cereal Treats

Recipe: Make a batch of rice cereal treats according to instructions on the box. Once cooled cut into rectangles. Melt chocolate in microwave (making sure to stir often), dip top half of cereal treat into the chocolate and quickly place candy eyes onto the chocolate. Let cool and enjoy!

Tattling	_Reporting_
• Accidental behavior	• Purposeful behavior
• To get someone in trouble	• Keeping someone safe
• Harmless	• Dangerous
• Unimportant	• Important
• If you can solve the problem	• Need help from an adult

Thankful Hearts (Thanksgiving)

Prayer

Song: #21 – "For Health and Strength"

Scripture: Colossians 3:15

Supplies: Autumn-colored construction paper cut into leaf shapes, rope or twine, mini clothes pins (sometimes these can be found pre-cut at local craft or scrapbooking stores)

Activity: Take turns saying something you are grateful for and writing it on a leaf cut-out. Hang the leaves on a garland or tape on a door/window and display through November.

Treat

The Song of the Heart

Prayer

Song: Free choice - This lesson is all about music, so you can skip an opening song if you like.

Scripture: D&C 25:12 and D&C 136:28

Supplies: Musical instruments (kid-sized instruments can be found on the party favor aisle at Target, Zurchers and Dollar Tree)

Activity: Explain to the children how we worship through music. Discuss what kind of music is appropriate. If any of the family plays a musical instrument, ask them to perform for the family. Let the children play music with the instruments while singing along to primary songs.

Treat

Tithing

Prayer

Song: #150 – "I'm Glad to Pay a Tithing"

Scripture: D&C Section 119

Supplies: Small boxes, decorations (foam stickers/glitter glue/pom-poms), blank tithing slip

Activity: Explain what tithing is and why we pay it. Show how a tithing slip is filled out and to whom we deliver it to on Sunday. Talk about what our tithing donations are used for. Make tithing banks for each child to store his/her tithing in each month.

* Often times small piggy banks can be found at the dollar store or Target for only a few dollars. Having an adult make a cut into the lid of a mason jar or an oatmeal canister also works as an easy and inexpensive bank.

Treat

Using Kind Words

Prayer

Song: #60 – "Jesus Wants Me for a Sunbeam"

Scripture: 2 Chronicles 10:7

Supplies: Tube of toothpaste

Activity: Have each person take a turn saying an unkind word while they squeeze the toothpaste out of the tube. After everyone has taken a turn ask each person to try and get the toothpaste back into the tube. Explain that once unkind words leave our mouth, they can be forgiven. But it is harder for them to be forgotten; That once the unkind words leave our mouth, they cannot be put back in again, just as the toothpaste cannot be put back in the tube.

Treat

Using our Talents

Prayer

Song: Your Choice

Scripture: Matthew 25:29

Supplies: Varies depending on each person's talents.

Activity: Discuss the talents you each have been given, and what you see other family members' talents as being. Then have a talent show!

*You may want to have this lesson span two weeks. On week one discuss how God gave everyone different and special talents. Then challenge each family member to prepare to showcase one of their talents on the second week at a family talent show.

Treat

Year End Review (Year End)

Prayer

Song: Your Choice

Scripture: 2 Nephi 25:23

Supplies: Interview sheets

Activity: Review your goals and family motto that was created at the first of the year. Then take turns individually interviewing each child/spouse and recording their answers. Store in a safe place to go back and re-read as you grow.

Treat

Year End Interview

Date:

Name:

Age:

Favorite color:

Favorite food:

Favorite memory of the year:

What I want to be when I grow up:

Favorite thing to do:

Favorite book:

Favorite animal:

What makes me happy:

Thanks, and love,

Heather Edwards

Instagram.com/heatedwards

heatedwards(at)gmail(dot)com

Made in the USA
Middletown, DE
31 October 2018